How a Decent Runner Can Get to the Starting Line at Boston-- in Spite of Himself

by

Gary Ishler

D1557210

Introduction

(Or Proof I May Have Clue)

Let me begin by saying I am a teacher, an English teacher no less, which unequivocally qualifies me as an author. However, you will judge that.

While this book is first and foremost about helping you, the reader, qualify for the most prestigious marathon on earth (outside the Olympics), the Boston Marathon, it is also about learning, specifically growing and improving from our mistakes, which in running are continual rites of passage.

What we do as runners is what we do in life: work hard, screw-up, correct those errors, and to our chagrin, keep repeating the cycle until there is no more work to do and no more blunders to make or correct.

That's when we are done. With running and all else.

There are many others who have written similar how-to books for qualifying for Boston, many teeming with scientifically-tested training and nutritional programs. This book doesn't offer that, per se. Rather, I present my personal experience as a runner for over 40 years who's qualified several times for Boston. Complete with my personal peaks and valleys, I hope that you may cull some useful points from the book, so my intent is to inform. But it's also to entertain—albeit at my own expense. I take my running seriously—too much so at times—but I don't really take myself seriously. I can be a lazy, clumsy klutz. Sometimes I wonder how I have managed to run so long, considering my penchant for getting in my own way.

Like many runners, I was lousy at team sports: too scrawny and not tough enough for football, couldn't hit in baseball, and I didn't care for basketball. All I could was run. Running opportunity at my small central

Pennsylvania high school was limited to a fledging track and field program. Sure, I could run 3-4 miles no problem, but fast? Not likely.

My running began as training for a backpacking trip to New Mexico. I started at a mile a day, and within a few months was up to three per day. I considered myself slow and never ventured into racing until I'd been running for about five years, then whimsically decided to run a 15K. I had been logging about 40 miles a week, and my longest run ever, prior to the race, was running the course two days before. I had never done speed-work-- didn't know what it was--but a 22 year-old can get by on youth and decent training. I finished second out of about 100 runners.

Two years later came my first marathon, followed by seven more in six years. Then, it was over a generation later--22 years--until I tackled another. But more on that later.

So what makes me qualified to advise, coach, cajole, or any other choice of appropriate verbs to get another runner to Boston? I consider myself a decent runner. Definitely not elite, not particularly fast, but better than average. My PR's, marks I set mainly during the Reagan administration, are okay—not worthy of any WOW's—but most runners would take them without hesitation. Considering I didn't start to take running seriously until I was out of college and ran that initial 15K in just over 53 minutes, including a 5:17 first mile, I thought at the time I had a little talent. Some of that might have been either unlocked and sharpened by a good coach, or left in a heap of ashes at the side of the road once I burned out. I know I have limits on how much I can do—Don't we all?—and I often push beyond them then pay the price. I'm not sure how I would have reacted to a coach, particularly one who pushed harder than I wanted to go.

Still, I can't complain too much about my running exploits, except that my PR's are now chiseled in granite. They will never change. That is the upshot of running young and having some success. Those who start later in life can PR in their 40's and 50's, but if you've been racing for decades, the best times come when young.

Now I can't change them even if I nuked all my scruples and went the Barry Bonds or Lance Armstrong route. It took me some time—one reason I didn't run a marathon again for so long because I'd be running against the former self I couldn't beat—to accept the reality that there is no chance I will run any faster, particularly at the short distances.

Yes, a longer running career sends PR's fading in the rear view, possibly because the legs might only contain so many quality miles. After a point, it's a struggle to get the same output. Much like a car, the more it's driven, the more its performance diminishes. Then the scrap heap. But if the mileage stays low, it has the ability to perform well for many more years.

I see many runners my age and older who are recording fantastic times, no doubt benefitting from fewer years and fewer miles. Even twenty years is a helluva lot less wear than double that. Eventually, the rigors catch up. Not that we can't run any longer, but the high quality will dwindle. Then it's a matter of just keeping one foot in front of the other (just like in the final miles of a marathon) and outlasting the others in our age groups.

As I lament my diminishing results, I take pride in my durability and consistency. Perhaps I'm lucky, too. At the risk of sounding boastful, I often mention how I have never missed more than a five or six days of running at a time due to injury or illness, and I can count those instances on one hand. Good biomechanics have been a blessing as well.

I'll be straightforward and acknowledge that while I am not a certified expert, be it a doctor, nutritionist, or guru-esque coach, there is science behind my tips, suggestions, and offerings. It's empirical evidence, the experience of four decades of running, volumes read, and coaching high school track and cross country. I don't have an attic full of lofty credentials and publication attributions, but—here's what's paramount--I HAVE QUALIFIED FOR BOSTON—then and now!

And that's the bottom line, or the finish line to properly complete the metaphor. Qualifying for Boston several times supports my claim to some degree of running decency, or for a better word, expertise. In my 20's, when the qualifying times were more demanding, it was quite an accomplishment. Not that it's diminished now, but I've only had to break 3:35 and 3:40 while in my 50s under the recent standards. Back in the 1980's, men 50-59 had to beat 3:20, a mark I've approached but not yet broken in my current decade.

I like to think I have qualified, generations apart, so to speak. My runs in 1987 and 1988 came when the standards were tighter, though more lenient than the prior 2:50 for men under 40, a time I was determined to break but never did.

I began running marathons in 1982, when I naively thought just running with little training would still get me to the finish line. It did—with some walking—in 3:37, a qualifying time for me now, but horrendous at 24, and ranking in the bottom half of most marathon fields back then. The next year, with virtually no training and intestinal issues throughout, I stumbled to a 4:20—just the slobber-knocking, snot-punch, ass-kicking I needed. The following year, I properly trained. Additional miles helped knock my 10K time down to 35 minutes, and with four runs of over 20 miles, my marathon was 3:00 flat. Over the next two years, I scraped more time off, getting the marathon down to 2:57 and the 10K to mid-34 minutes.

Better, but based on my times in shorter distances, my marathons were too slow. Certainly, time prediction charts are inexact, but they do offer insight into training deficiencies.

For example, in my case, the slower times for the marathon demonstrated too few miles. If, on the other hand, the marathon times are relatively faster than the half-marathon, 10K and 5K, then a runner isn't doing enough speed training. But those are very general observations. In running, no one rule applies to everyone. There is always a vast vagueness.

Nonetheless, some basic principles remain universal. To go faster, one needs to run fast in training. To run farther, one needs to run longer in training.

That's about it. Quite simple, actually, despite how complex we try to make it.

I like to believe that the best coaches aren't usually the superstars, but those who had to work hard to achieve some degree of success. The great ones often find it difficult to relate to those who are bereft of loads of talent. They may see it as easy. Not always, but think about how many hall-of-fame coaches and managers were hall of fame players. More often, the best mentors were those who did all they could with what they had while watching and learning from their own coaches.

I have learned much reading of great runners, gleaning advice from articles by and about them and their coaches, and just talking to other runners. We share a wealth of experience, good and bad, trial and error. What works for one may not for others. Training programs--no matter from whom--are largely cookie-cutter templates. Each runner must figure out—amid endless the experimentation—what works for him or her then adapt. And what works one year might blow up the next. Keep searching for answers because every one of us is a work in progress—as runners and as people.

So what makes this book different from others promising to provide the insight and enlightenment to help you run a Boston-worth qualifying time? For one, I have made a multitude of mistakes, probably even more as I've gotten older, in part by my refusal to accept declining performances.

Moreover, I offer an honest portrayal, a no embarrassment-barred chronicle of--as Shakespeare might describe it--"bloody, unnatural acts, of accidental judgments, casual slaughters."

Just to put your mind at ease, no one was casually slaughtered in the writing of this book. But because I love teasers, there will be some bloodshed--all of it my own.

Boston: Where Size May Not Matter but Time Does

A marathon is a marathon. Elevation and the size of the exploding number of events vary, but all are 26.2 miles. Still, while the distance is standard among all marathons, one stands out and rises prominently above all others, representing the Mount Everest of distance running. It is the marathon non-runners know, even if they have no idea how far it is.

It is Boston.

After I ran Boston in 2014, many people congratulated me on finishing. When I said that I didn't run as well as I would have liked but that I re-qualified for next year, their perfunctory response was, "Well, you finished."

As if there was any doubt!

In reality, had they known then, they should have congratulated me on qualifying the previous year at the inaugural Mount Nittany Marathon in State College, PA on a day when temperatures and humidity both climbed to near 90. Piling on the hardship, the course rose almost 800 feet in elevation. This was far from the perfect qualifier. Honestly, I never expected to qualify there. I wasn't sure if I'd even finish, but once I started and "chilled" (literally, I wish) the first half, I pushed the second half and qualified by 1:39. Not pretty but I made it into the Boston field by a mere second under the cut-off in a year when there weren't enough spots for about three thousand qualified runners. Qualifying was the real accomplishment—the cake, though no piece of one to get to the finish. Boston would be the icing.

Most non-runners are unaware of just what it takes to get to Boston. They aren't aware that the vast majority of competitors—those who truly deserve to be there—earned their numbers by running a prior marathon. And that was just to qualify. Most who run Boston don't qualify on the first try. For some it takes a few, a handful, or many attempts. Running Boston is a celebration. The hard work is in getting there.

America's oldest and most prestigious footrace has long been a destination for runners, even before the days of qualifying times. That added allure of having to qualify—while discouraging some—has motivated many.

Prior to the mid-1980's, before Boston relented to awarding prize money, the qualifying standards were rigorous. Men under 40 needed to break 2:50, while those in the 40's needed sub-3:10. It eliminated thousands—including me—who just couldn't run that fast. Seeing fields dwindling each year, the Boston Athletic Association eased qualifying somewhat—at least for younger runners—raising the threshold to three hours for those under 40. Since then, more time's been added, boosting the race numbers. The 1996 centennial race, with 38,000 strong, demonstrated that by breaking the race into separate waves and corrals, the B. A. A. could accommodate a field comparable to New York and Chicago. Thus, qualifying times became even less rigid.

That's also about the time that the concept of "Bucket Lists" came about, and running a marathon topped the myriad of accomplishments.

But not any marathon, mind you. It had to be Boston.

Consider that only about 10% of American marathoners are fast enough to qualify and that adds to the luster.

Now, if you think you're among the 90% not included, I must convince you to read the rest of this book and believe that you can be part of that semi-elite group. Have faith and pay attention. I can help get you there, or at least closer. But you must be willing to work hard.

Training for a marathon can be demanding and unyielding. Completing a marathon can be strenuous, sometimes tortuous. But preparing and qualifying for a Boston qualifier can be all that--squared. A BQ transforms the sum of all those parts to rewarding. Conversely, missing a qualifying time can be frustrating and demoralizing. Still, you can take it as a learning experience for next time.

I can't say qualifying is easier than it ever was, but there is certainly no shortage of training plans and self-proclaimed experts (including the one you're reading) offering ideas and insights.

Still, there are no guarantees. Your purchasing this tome will not assure you a BQ. But it might improve your running, it might improve your marathon PR, and it might provide a laugh or two.

Up until 2012, a runner could take advantage of a one-minute grace period. For example, if a man in his early 40's needed to run under 3:20, he'd actually have an extra minute, meaning his time just had to be under 3:21.

The less stringent times further heightened demand. The 2011 marathon sold out in eight hours. Many quality runners, some who had run the marathon for decades prior, were left out. As a result, the following year, the BAA revamped registration, allowing those whose qualifying times were 20 minutes or more under to register for the first two days. The next two days, it was those ten minutes or under, then five minutes, and finally those who just made it.

That year, it took about a month until the field of qualified runners (about 22,000 of the 27,000 with the rest charity runners) was filled. The 2013 race was similar.

Then there was 2014, when demand exceeded supply and about three thousand with qualifying times entered but didn't get in. I know how close that was. As mentioned earlier, I made it by a mere second. Registration for the 2015 race was nearly as competitive. That's the standard in the post-bombing era. In fact, the amount of money that the marathon generates for the greater Boston region on marathon weekend has increased 133% in the years since 2013.

Filling this Bucket (Or Just Deciding upon and achieving a goal)

Let me say this upfront: I detest the yuppie, trendy, term "Bucket List." I know it came from the movie of the same name, alluding to those places a person would like to go or things he or she would like to do before they kick the proverbial bucket, that is, a list of goals or accomplishments before one dies. I suspect calling them goals or aspirations is just too mundane, too ordinary. There needs to be flash and style.

So we're saddled with this irksome term "Bucket List," which has mutated into a tedious and tired cliché. Besides "Kick the Bucket," there's "Buy the farm," or take the "Dirt nap." Why haven't these other trivializing figures of speech ever garnered their own lists? Say, "Farm Chores" or "Nap Times." Presumably, the absence of a popular movie never let them catch on. Not that I would have been any more likely to use those epithets either, but they'd offer diversity, something against the flavor of the month. How's that for another cliché!

Running a marathon seems foremost on many of these lists, that is, life goals. And not just any marathon. Everyone wants to run Boston.

Why? It is the oldest marathon in the US with a history and tradition as rich as the city that bears its name. Within that heritage are layers of legend and lore, tradition and tales from the towns along the 26.2 mile route---Hopkinton and Ashland, to Natick, Wellesley, Newton, Chestnut Hill, and Brookline; the immortal landmarks--the starting line, Natick Common, Wellesley College, Newton Fire Station, Boston College, Cleveland Circle, the Citgo sign, Kenmore Square, the underpass...Boylston Street. And the legends themselves: Johnny "the Elder" Kelley, Tarzan Brown, Clarence DeMar, Bill Rodgers Robert Gibb, Katherine Sweitzer, Joan Beniot Samuelson, and in 2014, Meb Keflezighi. Many more international names have traversed the course in recent years, leaving their own legacies through the likes of Tishohito Seko, Ibrahim Hussein, Cosmos Ndtei, and Uta Piggig.

Everyone runner who crosses the starting line at Boston follows in the footsteps of hundreds upon hundreds of the greatest distance runners in the world.

Part of the allure of distance running, and major marathons in particular, is that the everyday athlete competes with the top names in the sport. What other event can offer that? Can weekend golfers play at the Masters, tennis players earn a seed at Wimbledon, or what bike rider has the opportunity to pedal down champs de elysee with the winners in the final stage of the Tour de France?

Adding further to the magnetism of Boston is the qualifying. Aside from the Olympic Marathon, Boston is the only one requiring runners to run under an age-specified time in a certified marathon during an approximate 18 month window. This allows a runner who qualifies in November to potentially use a BQ time for entry in the next two races, a quirk that didn't exist 20-30 years ago.

Running Boston graces a runner with a status unachieved in any other event. Everyone has heard of the Boston Marathon; it's familiar to the unfamiliar. Most outside the sport don't understand the qualifying procedure and that, as I said earlier, Boston is a marathon just like the one used for qualifying (although the topography of the course can be a quadriceps-wrenching challenge). But it's status and prestige rank it as the zenith of the sport. If people know you've run the Boston Marathon, you can expect to savor the afterglow of adoration for a few weeks following the race.

In New England, Bostonians and race spectators view the racers has heroes, though that title bears much a different connotation after 2013.

I recall after my first two Bostons, in 1987 and '88 the congratulations from the crowd. Part of that may have been the more elite nature of the much smaller field—5300 runners.

This was prior to bucket lists and less rigorous qualifying times. People would come up and ask, "Did you run the marathon?" An affirmative reply garnered a handshake or a pat on the back. It was a more personal display of support. With a field five and six times larger, the support now comes in the form of even more enormous cheering, raucous crowds along the course. Either way, there is no mistaking the passion the million or so spectators feel about the event and the runners.

Again, 2013 elevated that fervor and zeal to heights that now make Boston more appealing and enticing than ever.

All that said, qualifying for Boston doesn't take extraordinary talent, but there is a reason that only about one in ten marathoners make it there. Many, with the right training program, motivation and support can break through, but most can't. As hard as they may try, it doesn't happen. Honestly, they are just too slow. They simply lack the ability. How many of us dream we could be elite runners? One of my most fervent desires was to win the Boston Marathon—just once. Realistically, I knew it could never happen, which is why it will always be a flight of fancy. Kids grow up wanting to be stars in the NFL, NBA or MLB...maybe the Olympics. But most are left to dream and envy. Our country is based on offering everyone equal opportunity, but no one can grant us all inherent equal *ability*. It's also why some have the aptitude to become professionals like doctors and lawyers, and others are garbage men. This is not disparaging, just a fact of life.

As much as society (and running has become more and more guilty of this with medals for finishing 10K's and half-marathons, for example) tries to make everyone a winner, life doesn't play that way.

It's one reason why Boston has rigid qualifying standards. Without this winnowing process, the task of organizing the event would be unmanageable, and many quality runners would be left out (as was the case in 2011). There is nothing wrong with making people work harder to chase a goal. For those who achieve it, they deserve the accolades. For those who don't, they know they tried, and that drive and effort will make them better runners and better people. So never give up. My hope is to help you chase and perhaps realize that dream.

Just Qualifying is Not Running—Take it From Me, *Twice*

I: 2012--My Deferment Self-Indictment

Absent from Boston for 24 years, I was primed for the 2012 Boston Marathon. The training went well. I felt good enough to run sub-3:20. I started tracking extended forecasts three weeks in advance, as if there's any accuracy that far ahead. The Thursday before the marathon, the predicted high in Boston was 60-65 and sunny. A little warm, but tolerable.

Then Friday, the shock. Accu-weather called for a high of 85. From 65? What the hell, only my expletive was much more muscular than that!

That's it. I'm not even going. I can cancel the motel.

My wife (girlfriend at the time) said we were going. She'd packed, and even if I don't run, it'll be a mini-vacation.

I agreed and let the worry melt away. Wait and see. Maybe the forecast is wrong. I was incredulous over how it could have changed so radically, so quickly But unseasonable warmth was in store for Pennsylvania as well. Boston should be cooler, but...

We heard news of the deferment while browsing through a Barnes and Noble, my favorite retail establishment in the universe. A man in the store said he had heard about it on the news.

I was skeptical.

When we got back to the motel, I checked the B.A.A website, but didn't see anything. Maybe this was just a rumor.

Sunday, we went to the expo, I picked up my number, but no hint of deferment. Crowded and hot, we left the expo and sat at the Back Bay station, waiting for our train on a mid-summer Sunday--April 15.

When we arrived back, I had received the email explaining the deferment process. TV coverage of the marathon focused on the heat with the B.A.A. urging runners—particularly the inexperienced charity plodders at the back of the pack—to rethink this and sit it out.

I would wait until morning.

After a night of restlessness, I got up at five (I had to be on the train to Boston by six to catch the bus to Hopkinton) and stepped outside to a moonlight sky and comfortable temperatures. The only problem: it was five hours before the start and the sun wasn't baking yet.

I went back inside and crawled back into bed.

Uncomfortable already with my decision, I went out around eight for a run, about five miles to test out the heat. Even then, it was in the seventies. So I felt a little better about my decision.

We went into Boston to watch the finish in the midst of the bake oven. Spectators, crammed five or six deep on Bolyston Street, smelled as bad as the runners. Deodorant notwithstanding, 90 degrees in close quarters—even outdoors—will cause that.

But the olfactory offensiveness wasn't the worst of it. Witnessing the agony of the runners and the horrendous times—many well over 30 minutes slower than their qualifying times—should have helped me reconcile my decision earlier in the day. But it didn't.

Returning to the motel Monday evening—after a walk to Fenway Park—it also seemed as if the finishers were flaunting their achievements as they mostly limped around, their symbols of achievement hanging from their necks. I don't begrudge any of them. Finishing in that blast furnace, they earned it. Some displayed their hardware even after they had changed clothes and maybe showered. The medals still hung, and I regretted.

I don't remember showing off mine from the 80's quite that openly—if at all, but this is a different generation of marathoners, and that difference is what triggered much of my initial guilt then comfort then more berating then some solace, and on and on. The eight-hour drive home allowed me too much time to rationalize and second-guess. I drew far too many parallels with Hamlet over this, partly because I was teaching the play--my favorite piece of literature—at the time, and I tend to empathize with the protagonist as being far too analytical, like me. As if that wasn't already evident!

I had weighed the advantages of both sides. If I ran, I would have endured horrific conditions nowhere near what I had been experiencing in training—about 40-50 degree difference. The B.A.A. advised against running if not acclimated to the unseasonal heat, but only those from the South or nations in the Southern Hemisphere might have been accustomed to this inferno! In return for taking part in what was termed "an event" rather than a race, I dreaded being saddled with a sundial-timed finish after having trained for much better.

Much of why I didn't run a marathon for over 20 years was the realty that I couldn't come close to equaling times I ran in my 20s. Eventually, I came to the realization—age graded results helped—that I could never run as fast, but I could still train hard and smarter and do comparatively well— or better—for my age.

Running just for the medal and boasting that I finished would have been the only rewards. I had two medals, earned when the marathon's qualifying times limited it to more elite athletes, and I don't run marathons just to say I did them. Hell, I ran a training marathon in 3:28 two weeks prior to Boston. Moreover, I wasn't positive how my body would respond and subsequently react afterward. Deferring likely saved much stress, mostly from the heat, and allowed me to keep training.

Nonetheless, the most significant advantage was the spot for the next year. This avoided the need to re-qualify, which much of the 2012 field failed to do. In fact, after 43% re-qualified in the 2011 race, only 13% or just over 2700 runners did in the heat.

Looking back, I'm still ambivalent about my decision. I would like to have finished and earned the medal, but the end result might have been enough to forsake marathon running forever. Those who finished deserved the accolades. It was their day in the sun—a blazing, sizzling sun, no less.

II: 2013--Revenge of the Marathon Gods

(Or their masked blessing)

A year after my reluctant deferral from heat, I vowed that in 2013 year I was running, come Hell or high water.

The flu wasn't anywhere between those extremes.

After the incredulous, inexplicable, inexcusable and insane bombing at the race, some considered my flu fortuitous, that I avoided the melee that followed. Timing would have likely helped me get through the finish area close to an hour before the bombs went off. Of course, who's to say we might not have lingered around the area after I finished, though my plan was to get on the train as soon as I could.

Instead, it was all I could do to get out of bed to the bathroom in a suburban Boston motel.

But after running 2014 and knowing the length of time it takes to meander through the finish area, then wander to the family meeting area, wait for friends then shuffle to the train station, it's a couple of hours, so we might have still been in the eye of it, or at least nearby.

The flu, however, put the clamps to that.

Leading up to the race, I pushed the limit, and because I did, I felt confident I could break 3:20. Cranking out a nearly 70 mile week—the biggest of my training cycle— and a 3:24 full training marathon just over two weeks before Boston— compromised my resistance. I was ready to run. My confidence bordered on cockiness, in essence, Icarus flying too close to the sun.

I had avoided illness for four months, then five days before, the scratchy throat began and two days before, full-blown head in a pressure cooker to go with insatiable fatigue and chills. I never made it to the expo Sunday to pick up my number, and we left for home Monday morning, pulling out of the motel parking lot at 10:21, just about when I would have started in the second wave.

Once we had gotten to Scranton, my son called me to tell me about the blasts. He knew I wasn't running, but other friends and relatives didn't, thus igniting a barrage of text messages and phone calls to both my phone and my wife's. I should have taken heart to those who said, "It's too bad you got sick, but I'm glad you did." I appreciated the sentiment, but it didn't lessen my disappointment.

The tragedy was covered extensively, and I feel for all the victims and their families, particularly eight-year-old Martin Richard who had just hugged his father upon finishing the race. The attacks defied all reason and simple human decency. The mentality of murdering innocent people to advance radical beliefs should have no place in our world.

Two other runners from my local club did finish the race and managed to get out unscathed, but did get caught up in the ensuing bedlam after the explosions. One finished only nine minutes before the bombs went off.

When we arrived home that evening, I called them right away to see if they were okay. They wondered the same about me, since I never appeared on any of the race tracking. I was home, but so weak from not eating for two days I could barely make it up the steps.

I really had no desire ever to return to Boston again. In fact, as we headed home that morning, I told my wife, *I am never coming back here.* Lost money aside, the three days I just spent traveling there and back, and a day spent alternately roasting and freezing in a motel, combined for the worst trip I'd ever taken. One trip without running stung enough, but two?

Boston and I just weren't meant to be, at least not in this generation.

Ironically, for many the hard part is qualifying. But for me, that's been the easy part. The challenge has been getting to the damn starting line.

Because my running defines me, it raises my self-esteem when I'm doing well, and plummets it when I'm not. It was little wonder I sunk into a physical and mental funk. Not running Boston was akin to ripping out my heart. Getting sick flattened my physical well-being and shallow sense of invincibility that I never should have allowed to gain such a foothold.

As many reminded me of the fortuitousness of my getting sick, that someone was looking out for me, I refuse to accept that notion. It was not good luck in any way; just misfortune. Only those who have no clue how hard I worked can make such an assertion. They don't know the volume and intensity of training I endured for four months. Hell, even if I had known there would have been an explosion at the finish line sometime after three hours into the race, I still would have run. Terrorism wasn't going to deter me. Only the flu could do that.

Then again, I say that within the safe comforts of more than a year removed from that day.

When I suggested that I wanted to run in 2014, I was branded as crazy, and my wife made it plain that I was on my own (she wasn't totally serious). But I knew I must get this monkey off my back. Moreover, I want to be part of the return, of the Boston Marathon's display of resiliency and perseverance.

Boston's ability to bounce back was inspiring. The scene at Fenway the Saturday after the bombing and the day after one of the alleged bombers was captured demonstrated a celebration of the spirit and determination of the city, its people, its teams, and its marathon.

It would come back, and I intended to be back as well. Fortunately, Boston in 2014 was indeed the celebration it needed to be. And I made it to both the start and finish (though a little slower than I wanted).

I realize I should pack up the regrets like old trophies and move on. But I still can't. Materialistic I'm not, but I wanted that 2013 medal. The shirt would have been nice, being

41

able to purchase and wear the jacket would have been an honor as well, but I craved the hardware more. Maybe because I cherish those momentos I have earned, not bought.

Or maybe it's because I ran marathons long before finishing medals. Not until I ran Boston in 1987—my sixth marathon overall—did I have medal draped around my neck. And while I treasure those two Boston medals from days of yore, they pale in comparison to the race bling shining now.

Still, I go back to five Harrisburg marathons—two under 3 hours and no medals. I received certificates for the first few, but I don't recall getting one in 1985 and '86, my two fastest years (though I earned awards for age group places). Marathoners now expect a medal *and* certificate, regardless of finishing time.

One of the problems with our society today—and kids in particular—is that we have programmed everyone to believe there are no losers, an issue I touched on earlier. Everybody wins. Finish the marathon—seven or eight hours or so—and you're still a winner. Some would argue that completing the task is admirable, and I don't disagree; those runners should receive some recognition—a certificate, ribbon, whatever. But let's save the medals for those who have clearly worked harder to get there. A seven-hour marathon—unless it's the effort of someone in their 70's or above—demonstrates a lack of preparation. It is walking, not running. So why should someone who holds up the entire race machinery receive the same medal as a runner who finished three or four hours earlier?

Make medals a worthy reward. Cut them off at five hours, or some equivalent based on age. Those who don't make the cut-off still get something, but we need to distinguish between the runners and those out for a Sunday stroll. Medals ought to be earned, not handed out as tokens for showing up and crawling to the finish line.

I realize there are situations, such as Boston 2012, when weather greatly slows times. Again, a time limit, a runner limit, or whatever would be most fair. Each marathon could make that determination. Some may choose to medal everyone. That's their prerogative.

I just feel that medals ought to go to those who prepare and run the race.

I know this stance might infuriate many runners, particularly those who have come to the sport in recent years. I'm sorry, but a seven-hour marathon by an able-bodied runner under the age of 65 is a disgrace. I'd never want anyone to know I did it. I felt ashamed the year I ran Harrisburg—amid intestinal issues—in a slogging time north of four hours, a disgraceful time for a guy in his mid-20's. I was near the back of the pack. I deserved nothing! But that disaster motivated me. I trained properly, doing the requisite long runs, and the next year I ran three hours flat. Not rewarding every runner equally might motivate some to work harder the next time. Then when they do earn a medal, they can truly feel as though they accomplished something special.

Training and Qualifying

Enough—or rather too much--about me. This is about you, the reader, training for a marathon and earning a coveted Boston qualifying time. Here are the current times, courtesy of the Boston Athletic Association website. All standards below are based on official submitted net time.

Age Group	Men	Women
18-34	3hrs 05min 00sec	3hrs 35min 00sec
35-39	3hrs 10min 00sec	3hrs 40min 00sec
40-44	3hrs 15min 00sec	3hrs 45min 00sec
45-49	3hrs 25min 00sec	3hrs 55min 00sec
50-54	3hrs 30min 00sec	4hrs 00min 00sec
55-59	3hrs 40min 00sec	4hrs 10min 00sec
60-64	3hrs 55min 00sec	4hrs 25min 00sec
65-69	4hrs 10min 00sec	4hrs 40min 00sec
70-74	4hrs 25min 00sec	4hrs 55min 00sec
75-79	4hrs 40min 00sec	5hrs 10min 00sec
80 and over	4hrs 55min 00sec	5hrs 25min 00sec

Obviously, the younger you are, the faster you must run, and the less added time per every five years. One advantage (among the many disadvantages) of getting old—beyond 60--is an added 15 minutes every five years. Of course, that's much easier to achieve for the first year in the age group (say, 65) than the last year (69). One important piece of advice: Do not try to qualify for Boston in your first marathon, unless you are an elite runner who can relatively blaze through a half-marathon. Even then, there is no guarantee of a BQ unless you've done the mileage and long runs.

The marathon is an event that requires some seasoning. The first attempt is just to finish. Worry not about time. Just focus on running an even race and crossing the finishing line. Once that's done, then it's time to think about improving the time. It might take a few more tries--or several. Either way, every marathon is a lesson learned. There will be mistakes; just try to minimize them each time. Elusive as it might seem, there is a near- perfect marathon in each of us. That might be the one that gets you the valued BQ.

The more experience you have, the fewer weeks you might need, but 16 should be a minimum, and you should begin with a base of at least 20 miles per week. Most detailed training approaches also call for a long run and some form of speed training. Those are paramount components. Experienced runners often devise their own plans, but the majority prefer to adhere to one already laid out. The secret is finding that program, or a semblance of one, that works best for you.

One I found most useful during my first generation of marathoning came from former Olympian and current running/walking proponent Jeff Galloway. In *Galloway's Book on Running* from 1984—a book one I'd recommend wholeheartedly--he offered various plans tailored to those who just wanted to finish, to those with time goals from 2:38 to four hours (this was a time when a four hour marathon was pedestrian, not average, but also when there were fewer marathoners in their 50s, 60s and older logging slower times). All the recommended programs included a gradually increasing long run every other week, with at least four runs over 20, including—in the faster plans—runs of 28-30 miles. The weeks between the long runs featured mile repeats— working up to 12-- at faster than race pace.

I tried to follow Galloway's plan for a sub-three hour marathon but never made it to the 27- mile long run or 12 X 1 mile at 6:25 pace. Still, I managed three marathons under three hours in an eighteen month span, proof that it's possible to get by doing a bit less.

Aside from the long run and the mile repeats, Galloway's plans didn't advocate excessively high mileage— just a nine or ten miler every week— a day off each week (optional for the faster plans), and a second optional running-free day in lieu of a slow run.

No program is infallible. Each individual is different. I managed to reach my time goal without doing all the required work. That's important because if you become a slave to a program, you have no flexibility, and ultimately, if you make to the starting line, you might well be injured, burned out, or both. The experts who formulate these plans know that no one can stick to them 100%, so there is some leeway. Of course, these plans are just guidelines. With experience, a runner can be more eclectic, choosing the best components of varied approaches.

No matter which direction you choose, adopting someone else's plan or adapting to one of your own, you should strive for three major components each week: a long run, a tempo run, and a session that requires fast running.

But limit that fast running to no more than 20% of total weekly mileage. The remaining 80% should be slow and easy at a pace from 60 to 90 seconds per mile slower than race pace, and at times up to two minutes slower. This translates to about 75% of maximum effort. In short, run 80% of your miles at 75% percent effort and the remaining 20% of miles at 80% of faster. Slower running enhances aerobic development, and over 97% of energy used during a marathon is aerobic. (A test on the percentages comes at the end of the book!)

Strive to run a similar easy pace for the long runs, particularly in the latter stages of training, as the mileage gradually increases about every other week. Though I have done it many times, I do not-- under any circumstances-- recommend doing a 22 miler one week and a 24 miler the next. It's not intelligent training, and it is further evidence of my proclivity toward training stupidity. Another "Do as I say, not as I have done!" Sure, for a few outliers running 20+ miles on consecutive weeks is akin to short recovery runs to the rest of us. These are individuals who can complete marathons in consecutive weeks. They are freaks of nature or chemically enhanced. But almost everyone else needs sufficient time to recoup after the long runs. Rest and recovery don't get enough attention, but I know that as I get older, I know need more days off and more sleep to bounce back and maintain comparable performances.

I try to run tempo runs at the same pace as the mile repeats. These are about 25-35 seconds per mile faster than race pace. Generally, these tempo runs are only about 3-5 miles. Longer tempos—often in the second half of a long run—are obviously slower and closer to race pace, but usually faster than the recommended minute or so slower.

With intervals, try to vary the length, from 200 to 1600 meters, or mix in hills repeats. Do different workouts each week. Some runners grind out 800s every single week. Running the same length intervals every week does little for motivation, nor does it offer a chance to increase leg speed with shorter repeats, or improve sustained pace with longer variations. Variety is valuable in that it prevents burnout and dread.

I prefer to toss in assorted distances (usually comparable times on the road) with equal or shorter rests. Hills are a staple about every other week, again varying the length of the inclines, from those that might take 20-30 seconds to those requiring one to two minutes. This helps the legs adapt to diverse acclivities and degrees.

Runner's World touts Yasso 800s, repeats named after originator Bart Yasso. The idea is to start with four and run each consistently at a pace that looks like marathon time. For instance, if your goal is three hours, 30 minutes, then the repeats are 3:30, only in minutes and seconds. Some critics say the workout isn't that accurate, but when I've done them and tried to run the repeats in the 3:20 range, my marathon times weren't far off. The goal is to increase to ten repeats prior to the marathon.

While I prefer changing up each week, I do favor the longer intervals, and 800 is an ideal distance. I hate starting and stopping, and the longer length extends the lactate threshold. Research has shown runners training for long distances in particular derive greater benefits from the extended intervals. Respected coach and running guru Dr. Jack Daniels says three minutes is a suitable minimum length, which for most people would translate to an 800 at six-minute mile pace.

Where you do the intervals is a matter of personal preference. There is one school of thought that you can gain more consistency on a track. Or, like me, you may find you accomplish more on the roads, complete with the uphills and downhills you'll find in a race. Bear in mind, the elevation of each repeat (800's, for example) will alter your time. Use the pancake portions (as close to that flat as you can get wherever you train) to gauge whether you are where you should be.

Variance in speed training keeps it interesting, but it doesn't mean a runner must go overboard with these workouts every week. Depending on your goal, one day of speed-work might be sufficient. It might be all your body can tolerate. Two days might be asking for trouble in the form of overtraining or injuries, maladies of which I am all too familiar. Again, assess the percentages. If the tempo, interval or hill training exceeds 20% of your weekly mileage, cut back on the intensity.

One trait every runner needs is flexibility. Not the neuromuscular type—though that is important—but flexibility in training. This is how a runner can take a very generic training program, mix and match, tinker and toy, and make it work for him or her.

While training for the 2012 Boston Marathon, I tried a modified form of a three-day marathon training program, Just the idea sounds not only counterintuitive but loony!

My rendition called for running five days per week. The two added days were easy recovery, but generally, I did intervals or hills on Monday, ran easy on Tuesday, took off Wednesday, did a fast 10K pace tempo run (usually about 3-4 miles) on Thursday, took Friday off, ran a long run Saturday, and a short recovery run on Sunday. My biggest mileage week was just 47, and I averaged only about 40 miles per week. But

I completed four runs of over 20 miles—21, 23, 24, 25—and ran all of them between 7:45-7:55 pace. I was aiming for a sub 3:20 marathon, so I only had to ratchet up the pace another ten seconds per mile to do it. That might seem too fast for long runs, but I felt strong throughout. Of course, I didn't run the marathon—and would never have been close to my goal in the heat that day.

But the following Saturday, after I spent a week mentally upbraiding myself for not running Boston, I unleashed my vengeance and aggression in a 24.2 mile training run in 3:05—and the last 1.2 was a slow cool-down. Confident I could run two more miles in fewer than 16 minutes, the effort confirmed my belief that I was in 3:20 shape. All I had to show for it, however, was the time on my watch.

My program violated many principles of virtually every other, including the notion that the long run should not exceed about a quarter of the weekly mileage, not half of it. Or knocking out two speed sessions per week. But it worked for me. That's the fundamental truth in training. What works for some, won't work for others. There are the majority opinions, but also many unconventional options, such as the three-day a week program, or the Hanson's 16 mile longest run. Many runners use these programs and are successful. One side does not fit all.

That is why you should research programs and tailor them to your own situation and capabilities. I have never been able to do excessively high mileage. In my 20's I peaked at 70-75, with several weeks over 60, but ultimately, I averaged about 55 per week. My body couldn't handle any more. I'd fatigue and have to cut back. I know from 2013 that my overtraining two weeks prior to Boston was my Waterloo. There is always a fine line between fit and worn. Each person must determine where that line lies. No training plan, no coach, no trainer, no fellow runner can tell you where it is. And the only way you discover it is through your own pitfalls and successes. Experience is your paramount guide. The longer you run, the more you know and understand about your abilities and limitations--if you think you have any.

Training for marathons in your 20's and 30's allows for a much heavier load than in the 40's, 50's and beyond. The more seasoned body can't take the same pounding. While I basically took what I did when younger and modified it based on experience and what I could realistically do 25-30 years later, I did look for some programs that at least confirmed my desire to get more quality without interminable quantity. The five-day plan I described earlier fit my capabilities well.

I also stumbled upon a program at coolrunning.com. The site offers reasonable programs, divided by beginner (4:00), advanced (3:30), intermediate (3:00) and competitive (2:30). The program, even the beginner template, advocates at least four long runs, culminating at 26 miles. That's during a week that tops out around 45-50 miles, another violation of that stupid axiom that the long run should only be about 25% of the total week's mileage. The beginner and intermediate programs list one day of speed or hill training, one day off, and runs generally in the 4-7 mile range, all at 90 seconds to 2:00 slower than race pace. Easily one of those shorter runs could be dumped in favor of a rest day, especially for an older runner. Like me.

In my years of running I have come to one conclusion: I hate speed work. Not that I don't do it, but I dread it. I know most runners share that sentiment. It's a necessary evil, one that we endure then paradoxically feel a sense of relief and euphoria at having completed it.

Age aside, one will not get distance-fast on intervals alone, even the longer repeats. That's why tempo runs are so effective. There is one workout that will work for anyone of any ability, building strength, speed and confidence—skills and traits needed to run a BQ marathon. This workout is a staple of my training. I have dubbed it the *Progressive, Negative Split, Race Pace Tempo Run.* The run fulfills the need for the tempo run and makes up for those weeks when I blow off the interval training. This run is just what the long-winded name says it is. Obviously, it works best for training from the 10K to the marathon but can also build speed and endurance for the 5K.

This run is most effective when logging six miles or more. The approach is simple: Run fairly easy for most of the first half (for me at least four miles until I am loose, a distance that grows longer as I grow older), gradually increasing the pace as you approach the halfway point. From that point, strive to hold goal pace for whatever distance you're going to race. I have used this run to prepare for marathons, cranking the second half of a 25-miler at my intended pace for the whole race. Except I am a notoriously slow starter, explaining how I manage second half splits sometimes ten minutes faster than the first half. It is negative splitting to the extreme. I like to think it's smart running, but sometimes I am too careful and cautious. I usually run well, but wind up a minute to two short of my goal because I become more conservative than Rush Limbaugh (but Rush and running are quite antithetical).

This workout also remedies the inevitable slowdown most runners endure near the end of a race. Further, training for the second half generates a mental toughness and late race confidence. Do this work-out twice a week. One of the workouts may be part of your long run. But don't forsake one interval or hill workout per week. That will help build the leg speed for late in the race.

As I stated previously, I'm not advocating any specific programs. Just the amalgamation of ideas and suggestions I've described in no particular order. Not that all or most will work for you, but if you're seeking a BQ without burying yourself in undulating mileage, some of these recommendations and workouts can be of value. Overall, it might be less—or even more--than you planned. So by all means, modify as needed. No single program is personally tailored, unless you pay gobs of money and hire some unseen personal coach who'll send you workouts via e-mail. But, having been a coach, I know it takes time to know your athletes—their goals, desires, work ethic, work capacities, and the one often overlooked—heart. I've witnessed high school runners brimming with talent and work ethic, but when it came time to demonstrate sheer guts, they timidly withdrew into a shell of surrender, intimidated by someone they perceived as better. Not backing down might not win the race or earn you a BQ, but it demonstrates a mettle that makes a statement and commands respect. It will serve you well in the future, be it in running or life.

Marathon running is certainly not for the sheepish. It takes guts to commit and train, and it takes heart to finish. The amount of heart one shows in reaching that finishing line—in a BQ, no less—is immeasurable. Any coach would be proud.

That said, I'm not your coach—just an experienced advisor-- but if you have a spoonful of talent and a gallon of that aforementioned heart, you can do this: YOU CAN GET TO BOSTON!

Just remember to mainly do as I say, not so much as I have sometimes done.

Hill or Hell?

Hill or Hell? Is there a difference? Shouldn't rising higher imply something far more ethereal?

Or is the suggestion of going higher just a ruse, a temptation that actually suggests moving in the other direction.

There's likely a valid reason why the words hill and hell are just a vowel apart. To some runners, they are one in the same. To totally twist the analogy, hills are essentially—to abscond with another Christian allusion--the Holy Grail of running. Few experts would dispute it. I hearken back to Frank Shorter's line to the effect that *Hills are just speed-work in disguise*. Not only speed, but strength and power, physically and psychologically. Constant hill work may not level out the incline (only heavy equipment can do that) but it will provide some ease in ascending it. That breeds a level of confidence in races when most runners consider hills drudgery, pain, and outright torture. Those are the ones walking up.

Hills are vital in marathon training, no matter whether the course features a net elevation rise or drop. Even the most downhill courses (like Boston or Steamtown in Scranton, PA) get in the act with a few inappropriately placed ascents in the closing miles. Steamtown's infamous hill at 25 miles is particularly grating. Running that far then staring at not a steep, but long, gradual rise that seems to go on forever is demoralizing and, some would say, even sadistic. The only thought is the finish can't be too far. While late hill placement seems inhumane after nearly a 1,000 foot elevation drop, the most effective way is prepare and include acclivities in training.

When I coached high school track, hills were imperative to our success. Though the kids didn't particularly like them, they quickly realized the benefits. When we did repeats on inclines that ranged from 100 to 300 meters, they'd want to know how many before we even started. *Ten or fifteen,* I told them, choosing to see how they responded. If many struggled, I could back off the workout, but if they were running well, attacking the hill with solid form, I'd let it go. Usually we'd run for time, around 20-30 minutes so the better runners accumulated more repeats and the slower, fewer. The telltale sign to back off came when one or two of the notorious retchers on the team starting spilling their cookies--a not uncommon occurrence among some members of the team who created and proudly wore t-shirts that read *If you ain't pukin', you ain't tryin'*.

Selling hill workouts wasn't easy, particularly to new freshmen runners who saw upper classmen bent over alongside the road. Nonetheless, I did have a core of runners who really bought in. Of course, I did the workouts with them, and a few times I attached myself to someone I thought needed a push. Not that any of them really liked it. At 51, 52 years old, I couldn't stay with the one or two fastest runners, those running sub 2:05 800's or sub 4:40 miles, but with a small team and fewer than a dozen distance runners, I could outrun most of them.

One of the better runners I could stay with didn't have the best form. So I ran beside him, encouraging, and matching step for step. I didn't admit it, but he was getting the best of me. Who was I to give in? I never wanted them to do it, why would I, despite giving away 35 years--a fact I often reminded them about. His coach on his shoulder, his form improved and soon he was kicking my ass: motivated to beat the old man. Whatever it takes.

We were fervent about hills, doing them at least once a week, and even incorporating a fairly steep 150 meter punch-to-the-face at the start of a 1000 meter residential area loop that even state qualifiers could manage only to finish 4-5 times in one workout.

During training for my first Boston runs, I heard the horror stories of Heartbreak Hill so I vowed to be prepared. Starting at three, I gradually built up to ten repeats on a quarter- mile hill that I have run thousands of times. It worked. I barely noticed Heartbreak, then, that is. Twenty-seven years later, it did get my attention, but it wasn't as daunting as hills in Pennsylvania can be.

Yes, hills do wonders. Just make sure you choose hills that aren't so steep that crawling is the preferred method of reaching the top. Form is crucial—into the ground with the toes, slight forward lean, head up and elbows churning. Vary the length and pace: faster on shorter hills, and slightly slower on the longer versions. Do them once a week, as a speed session or as strides on a slight rise at a slightly slower pace.

No matter what marathon you choose as a qualifier, hills will help get that BQ. And when you get to Boston, they'll help you through the Newton Hills starting at 16 miles and through Heartbreak (the least lethal of them all) at 21.

But it's not just uphills that leave many a runner writhing on a road. Downhills can be even more devastating. They tear up the quads, hammer the knees, and render legs to Jello, overcooked spaghetti, or any other substance approximating a lack of any consistency. In essence, mush. Though the declines can pound the legs into oblivion, it's only temporary. By minimizing the muscles to this congealed state, they eventually solidify and strengthen. They may do a quick 180 and petrify to stone or cement the next day, but keep it up, and you will have formed something akin to an unbreakable rope that will expand and contract when you need it—up and down.

Not Knowing When to Say When

As I have gotten older, I find that the hideous manifestation of overtraining stalks and ravages me more often, as often as once a training cycle. The classic symptoms are fatigue, legs with no snap or no freshness, and running that feels more like a detestable job--a necessary drudgery. Of course, those of us who must face this ugly menace have no one to blame but ourselves.

Overtraining results from too much mileage and/or speedwork, and too few rest days, an under-appreciated component of which I find I need more, and feel better when I build them in. But there is that Puritanical conviction that too many days off is slothful; more miles means more fitness, and after all, I did more miles than this for the marathon I ran a year ago and I didn't feel this bad then. One day off per week ought to be sufficient. It was for me 20, 30 years ago. Reluctantly and realistically, however, I have to acknowledge that advancing through the 50s, the body needs more respites, more days to recover and rebuild. Part of it is the nature of the workload, but some of it is just the cumulative effect of decades and decades years of running. As the miles accumulate, we all slow down, some sooner than others. And the body—legs chiefly among them—need more time to rebound.

That doesn't make me feel any less of a slacker. That's what I need to accept, but I have difficulty with it. Credit my wife, in the midst of one my annual summer overtraining, burnout spells, for stating the obvious, so apparent that I was either impervious or ignorant. *You're running more miles and you're getting slower. Shouldn't that be telling you something?*

My wife is also a runner, not a racer, through she occasionally takes on a flat 5K . She's never run or trained for marathons, but she knows if she goes beyond her customary 4-5 days a week and 20 or so miles, her body starts to tell her. Bodies are good at that the older we get.

There is no crime in taking an unscheduled day off if you feel stale. Maybe take two in a row. As much as I loathe doing that, I must admit, it's usually restorative, both physically and mentally, returning a proverbial spring to my step.

If you've allowed yourself to plunge into the overtraining abyss, falling ill or injured, then it might be time to take off more days. Some experts recommend up to a couple of weeks, depending on the severity of the overtraining and accompanying maladies. Again, I find that just cutting back to four days in a particular week helps tremendously, that is, until I undo the benefits and jump right back into the running six, or seven days per week. That's because mileage is power. The more miles I put in, the higher my average of a week or two, the more I can brag about it in my log book and to others. (but not on social media, a trend that is blatantly narcissistic). Given time, it all comes back to bite me, sometimes sharper and deeper than before. One rest day usually does the trick, provided I only run another day or two before I rest again.

By rest days, I mean just that. Squeezing in 3-4 miles is not a rest day, no matter how slow. Save those runs for the days after long, hard efforts, and stick to a pace up to two minutes slower than marathon pace. It might be a plod worthy of a tortoise, but who cares? (Hey, he beat the hare and they didn't even run a marathon!) Every day is not to be for speed.

Here's a simple running aphorism many of us—me included—conveniently ignore: Run the hard days hard and the easy days easy.

Marathon training requires ardent physical and mental investments. As a result, when the body gets tired, the mind might not be far behind. It's time to take a hiatus, back off, lest Overtraining Syndrome, a distressing plague that grabs you by the throat and doesn't let go. Otherwise, recovery and a return to training might take weeks, months, or even a year, depending on how long you have allowed yourself to sink into the overtraining clutches. The secret is being able to head off that level of physiological fatigue before it fully erupts. Don't upbraid yourself for a day off, or even two. That might be the refresher your need. If not, take more time. Basically, take what time you need for however long until running is fun again—or at least going out doesn't feel akin to a daily trip to the dentist for a root canal.

For all my misdeeds, mistakes and misfortune, I have been lucky in one respect: I have managed to run consistently for almost 40 years free of any major injuries. I am most proud of that longevity. Few others can make that claim. That doesn't mean every run has been pain-free and there haven't been many, many pulls, strains and other assorted ailments along the way, from shin splints to hamstring pulls, to piriformis syndrome (which feels like sciatia), to Achilles bursitis, to nueroma, to patella tendonitis. Some are more memorable because I've dealt with them in the past five years—one of the millions of casualties of not only getting older as a person, but as a runner. Luckily, I have avoided more debilitating infirmities. None of the injuries I experienced was serious or painful enough to stop me from training for more than a few days—at most. Regardless of the discomfort, I had to run. It's the addictive part of the sport, and as much as I sometimes I wish I could grant myself an extended break, I know I can't. I've been at it too long. The effect may not be as habit-forming as a narcotic, but it's close. A week without running and I'm clawing at the walls like a caged cat.

I first heard about notion of running addiction in the 1970's. I 'd only been running a couple of years at the time, and only a few miles a day, but I could relate to the idea of *needing* to run rather than *wanting* to run. And what addiction is complete without a high? Thus, the concept of runner's high—a euphoria that kicks in after about 30 minutes. I can recall many of those experiences, but honestly, not in the past 25 years. There were runs when I enjoyed those illuminating moments when my legs flew and I felt nothing could stop me. Not so much now, as the only sensation resembling a high comes when I'm done running. Then it's, *Thank goodness!*

Addiction takes holds rapidly, and needless to say, if you're running marathons and training for Boston, you're hooked. If you think that after you run Boston, you'll retire or step away for a time, satisfied with your accomplishment, think again! Boston's an even stronger enslavement. The crowds and atmosphere are intoxicating. You want more. Why do you think so many return year after year?

The sure way to escape the hold running and marathons have on you is to get hurt. Talk to former runners, those forced to stop due to injury, and unequivocally all will lament their inability to still run. This is particularly true among marathoners because they are the most dedicated, the ones who have sacrificed the most to reach their goals. Yes, they miss the rewards, but also the work, and how good they felt. But getting hurt and suffering serious enough physical issues to sideline them for good is the toxin that terminates the addiction, though not positively.

I've often thought that injuries might be preferable to overtraining. One might prevent the other. But I can rebound much quicker from being fatigued than I can a knock-me-off the-road-for-an-extended-time injury.

Getting Out of My Own Way

Busy lives and a tendency to over-train have spurned some marathon training programs that tout the value of fewer running days per week. In fact, the publishers of *Runner's World* have been promoting a three-day per week training program that features specific plans for all 16 Boston qualifying times. When the program says three days per week of running, that's what it means. But the three days are-- you guessed it--long run, tempo, and interval/hill training. And all three days are intense. Among the remaining four days, runners are to engage in some form of cross training, BUT NO RUNNING!

Cross training might involve anything from weights to swimming and biking. Whichever, it might actually trigger more injuries that running. At least for me.

Plyometrics is one form that has caused me consternation and hurt. When I first started doing these, I launched into a series of broad jumps in my backyard, and I noticed immediate results. My legs felt fresher and faster. Until I did one hop too many and strained my lower back, an injury I suffered almost once a summer, sometimes the result of not even knowing what I did. This torment provides a preview of what it will be like when I'm 90. No lateral movements, only straight ahead. During most of these back injury curses, I can run if I keep it short, slow and don't veer from a straight line. Typically, though, I have to rest and let the back heal, with the help of a heating pad and Doan's pills-- or the OTC equivalent.

Needless to say, I modified my plyometrics to leaps on a step or box. But they result in sore knees on the jumps down. To avoid that, experts recommend just stepping down then jumping back up. If I had any sense of self-preservation mode, I might have figured that out.

Those who don't fall shall fall. So it was with my foray into biking. In 1990, I purchased a road bike with tires thinner than African marathoners. It offered about as much tread and traction as ice. Cycling was a welcome diversion from running a couple of days a week—10-20 miles each ride--when the weather allowed. I discovered two things about biking. First, I'd rather run uphill than bike uphill, generating a whole new respect for those "clean" cyclists –oxymoron that it is--who scale the peaks in the Tour de France. When I would ride with experienced cyclists, I was always bringing up the rear, a good mile behind. My only solace came in knowing I could outrun them.

My second conclusion about biking is merely an axiom that all who pound two wheels share: those who haven't wrecked will. My first mishap was minor—failing to get my feet out of the toe clips at a stop sign. I wasn't moving so the plop on one side wasn't bad.

But a one significant wreck sent me to the ER. Again, due to my own stupidity. On a hot, humid Sunday, I started out with a t-shirt, but shed it a few miles into what was to be about 15 mile ride. I stuck the shirt in the back of my shorts, but it worked its way into the back wheel, clogging the brake clamp and grinding the bike to an abrupt halt. It hit the pavement and smacked me down, scraping my right side for at couple of feet. Unsure what happened, I picked myself up to find blood running down my shoulder, elbow and knee—

basically, the raised areas. The road rash burned, but not like my hip, which I concluded was broken. The area was very rural, but a woman who lived in the nearby house, complete with box seats to my mishap, came out and asked if I was okay. I never would have admitted I wasn't. I surveyed the damage to the bike and pulled the shirt, complete with several black, oily blotches on it, from the rear brake. I climbed back on the bike and headed home, bloodied and with a hip approaching rigor mortis. For fear of embarrassment and ridicule, I didn't divulge details on how the accident occurred to my then-wife, but as I lay on the couch at home, the hip locked up so tight I could barely move. It was worse than after a marathon by quite a stretch. The ER x-rayed, put some suave on my wounds, and gave me a tetanus shot, a staple for those prone to such bouts of road rash. I expected a broken hip, my running career shattered like Bo Jackson's football career less than a year earlier. When the doctor came to discharge me, she wasn't at all forthcoming about my injury. Of course, it was broken, she'd tell me, so I concluded it must be less severe, but every bit as excruciating.

"The hip--was it a bruise?"

Yeah, that's all. Or something to that effect. Emergency doctors are like those in *M*A*S*H*, depicted as meatball surgeons. ER is like factory medicine. Except the machinery at this factory usually breaks down and you wait and wait and wait and wait. And so on.

Sleep that night was impossible, as was getting to work the next day. Getting in and out of the car would be out of the question. Moreover, I couldn't do stairs, and there were two flights to the radio station studio where I worked. In fact, even a small upgrade on the crosswalk outside was a formidable obstacle. Gradually, the hip loosened, but I couldn't run. I needed some hair of the dog, get back on the bike, which I did, trepidation not withstanding with some white-knuckling on the downhills. By the end of that week, I needed to run. The first mile was nursing home pace, but as I went, the steel bands of tightness in the hip started to soften, and by mile three, I barely noticed.

That foray into cycling injury didn't totally end my riding, but I didn't have the same desire afterward. Eventually,

I sold the bike for about a quarter of what I paid for it. I'd like to bike again, remembering to keep the shirt on. And, by the way, the next bike may have tires fatter than a sedentary American.

I didn't have a major problem with falling while running until I went minimal. I'm not sure if there is some correlation between the front of the foot landing as opposed to the heel that produces a more likely probability of crashing. It is why I have never done much trail running, particularly on what those in that sport refer to technical, euphemistic for damn rough: boulders, goonies, stones, roots, logs, swamps, streams, and cliffs that make crawling as close to running as one gets. Plus, downhills so precipice that rappelling would be a far more effective and safer means of descent. So I hasten to think how I might emerge from a trail run. Roads are bad enough.

That truism that applies to bikers should also apply to runners: those who haven't fallen, will. Think about it, every run presents innumerable obstacles that with some slight step askew, down you go. I've fallen and wound up with the palms of my hands, elbows, knees and face bloodied from turning ass over tin cups as a result of catching my toe in the lip between the pavement and berm, tree branches, pieces of wire, and the predictable snow and ice, though counter intuitively, the penchant toward caution when it's slick usually keeps me upright.

Even worse than the cuts and scrapes are the pulled muscles (rib cages easily aggravate with every turn and take weeks upon weeks to heal).

But most humiliating is the act of falling itself, a mishap non-runners fail to understand and find hilarious. Especially if they happen to be driving by when you tumble. Stop and help, forget it. Laugh like hell—you bet!

My most hilarious fall—though definitely not for me—came about six weeks before the 2013 Boston. I should have recognized this calamity for what it was—a horrific omen for the marathon and for me. I was a half-mile from home, about to turn into our development, and finishing the final cool-down mile of 18 on a blustery Saturday morning. Just before the turn, there is an intersection where the off-ramps and on-ramps of a four-lane highway meet. After I ran through the underpass, I hopped up on a concrete median that tapered to a point. When I go to the end of it, I took the step down onto rumble strips. I thought the step was about a foot—the height of a curb. I underestimated. It was closer to two-feet (I've never ventured out to measure it). When I went down, one of my toes caught in a groove on the concrete, and I planted face first. I'll never forget the "Oh, shit" reaction as I put my hands out to try to stop the fall, but the force sent my nose and forehead into the wedge between the strips. That was my saving grace. Had I smacked into flat concrete, I likely would have suffered a concussion and much more bleeding—much to the uproarious delight of the sadists driving by, none of whom stopped to check on me. After impact, and fearing that I likely broke most of my face, I popped up, wiped my ungloved hand over my mug to survey the wreckage. There was blood but not gushing volumes that I feared. And none from my nose, even though the tip of it came in direct contact with the unforgiving surface. I crossed to the right side and hightailed back the development, hopeful that no one else would witness the aftermath of this atrocity for fear that while on the run I'd been attacked. Actually, I had been. Who the hell says running isn't a contact sport? When I got inside the house, I went right to the bathroom to further assess my defacing. Blood on the nose, above the bridge of my nose and my forehead. Not nearly as bad as I feared. But when I walked in the kitchen, my wife laughed. Not "Are you okay?" No, humor. Eventually, once she composed herself, she did ask what happened. The story itself elicited more amusement then direction to get anti-biotic on my copious wounds. And, she speculated, I would probably have one or two black eyes.

I hadn't thought too much about the impact of my appearance. I knew I'd have to bandage some of the spots, like the bridge of the nose—that was the worst. Most of the wounds were scrapes, which are often more widespread and hideous looking than deep wounds. I hoped I'd be healed soon. I usually recover quickly. But it wouldn't be quick enough for my grandson's birthday party the next day. I had to answer plenty of questions about what happened, and I'm sure some people had a few laughs—if they weren't grossed out. I tried to cover the worst, but the Band-aids didn't stick real well with the Neosporin underneath, so I kept making sure the one on the bridge of my nose stayed put. I was sure my ex-wife would revel in my misfortune and injury. Fortunately, she stayed at an opposite end of the room. Not that she didn't witness my ravage, but contained any glee she may have felt.

I considered a sick day from school just because I didn't want to give my students both the view of the face minus epidermis or reason to mock me. Never mind that I could match wits with any of them (a statement on their plentiful lack wit rather than my abundance of it). I chose to approach it head-on—pun intended! Diffuse the situation with self-deprecating humor. If I make fun of myself, that doesn't give anyone else much to work with. Those who do ridicule themselves are viewed as more worthy of support and even sympathy.

Of course, the observation skills among many of the kids were as deficient as their wit. As they filtered into the room, some gave me looks similar to those who first saw the

Frankenstein monster. There were some truly concerned: "Mr. Ishler, what happened?"

"Long story, but you should see the other guy."

Most of them truly believed I'd been in a rumble. Did I mention they're also gullible?

I knew it was best to share with them the gory details, interspersed with digs at my own stupidity and appearance. By the end of the day, I had rehashed the story for five more classes and numerous colleagues who had apparently colluded on the question they would ask: *What happened to you?*

Gradually, the wounds healed, leaving a few surfaces blemishes that dissipated with time. I went right on training, quite well, almost forgetting my median kiss, except when I drove by it and cursed the bastards who put it in and designed it. I was past the self-deprecation stage, opting for good old American rationalization and blaming of someone else.

But on April 13 when I collapsed on the bed at the Econo-lodge in Sharon, Massachusetts feeling as if I didn't hit a concrete medium but a high-speed locomotive, I realized that only I was to blame for my carelessness resulting from my perceived invincibility—and genuine stupidity.

Eating & Training

(Doing One to Justify More of the Other)

One of the heralded benefits of marathon training is the perception that food is everything. Run to eat, not eat to run. Subscribe fully to that mentality to the excess and less than sensibly, and you might well spend much of the race searching out port-a-johns, as I have done a few times.

I learned eating greasy pizza at eleven o'clock the night before the marathon isn't smart. That led to some gastrointestinal issues that claim credit for a stellar 4:20 effort in my second marathon in 1983. I also battled some minor GI problems in a 2:57 BQ run three years later that would have been faster if not for that stop at eleven miles. The worst came in 1988 when I suffered stomach cramps that almost doubled me over and left me ready to quit halfway. Thankfully, I endured and actually ran 43 minutes for the final 10K, finishing in 3:06—despite walking about two miles.

A side note: not necessarily for those reasons (life— translated into kids, work, divorce, career change, return to college—got in the way) that was my last marathon for 22 years.

I'm not sure what triggered the aforementioned stomach problems, but I do know my diet then, in my indomitable 20s and early 30s, was to eat whatever I wanted—and drink copious amounts of beer. My weight held around 165-170, which kept me strong. Eat and drink prodigiously and run it off. What you can get away with when you are young!

It's another of those situations where if I had only known then what I know now, how much faster I could have run.

By the time I ran another marathon in 2010, I was about 20 pounds lighter, eating healthier, though still indulging in too many sweets. Going through a divorce contributed to much of the weight loss and renewed dedication to training. That led to wins over small, slow fields in several 5K's in my mid-40's when I could still break 18 minutes. Suffice it to say, once I got serious about marathons and more long, slow distance, those times bloated to 19 and 20 minutes.

I also started to pay a little more attention to what I ate, but I can't say I adhered to what nutritionists recommend: 60-65% carbohydrates, 25% protein, and 15% percent healthy fats. I still don't heed those recommendations very much. I do read labels for calories, fat content and protein. I don't eat enough protein or healthy fats. In fact, I am one of those who used to believe no fat was the way to go. Never mind the carbs and sugar. Twizzlers and Mike and Ike's candies were perfect foods—no fat. Run enough and the glycogen from the sugar will ignite and burn like dry leaves. Fortunately, I have modified that somewhat. I cut out the Twizzlers.

As I approached 50, my goal was to be in the best shape of my life. I didn't necessarily run more miles. I wasn't doing marathons at the time, so 30-35 miles per week was suitable for running 5K's in the 18:30 range. But I knew my diet need such adjustments, so I began adhering to a few rules:

1. No fried foods
2. No soda
3. No white bread
4. No beer

I had curtailed my indulgence in # 4 about five years earlier. I estimated I had drunk my fair share during my twenties (when I logged my best times—must have been the carbs) but I did start to worry that I might be swigging too much brew. Over time, consumption dropped to virtually nothing. Now, the mere whiff of beer makes me want to retch.

I've found that the longer one goes without a food that had formerly been clogging a diet (and likely arteries), the more a person despises that particular item and not only doesn't want it anymore, but wishes it was banned due to its detriment to everyone's health.

Such is the case with soda. I drank enough of most every brand, but had a particularly affinity for Mountain Dew. The Code Red version was my soda of choice before I quit. This was also a gradual withdraw, as I had whittled consumption to about a third of a 20 ounce bottle every other day. What's the use? I asked. I kept a bottle in my desk at school for lunch, but many days didn't even take a sip. At the end of the school year, I finished the few remaining swallows and stopped altogether.

Ridding fried foods and white bread came even easier. My fried choices were limited to fries, but I only ordered them when eating out, and there are usually far better choices. Bread was never a staple. I ever cared much for sandwiches. Toast was just burnt bread, and idea of mopping up a meal with a slice of bread reminded me of a janitor slopping up a dirt floor with a mop. That is not to say I don't eat my fair share of bread in certain restaurants, which as Olive Garden and a ubiquitous chain of central Pennsylvania eateries known as the Original Italian Pizza, whose bread may be the best anywhere.

There are a few items not on the list that I may grab when I'm in a celebratory mood, such as after completing a long run or a marathon. Ice cream, potato chips, cake—just to name a few. But I don't eat them often. If I did, I might weigh 250 instead of 150.

Cheat days are the latest mechanism for eating what you what, without depriving yourself and totally unraveling any self-discipline. That's not to say we should plunge into full, unbridled gluttony for 24 hours. It's a way of relaxing the limits you put on yourself the rest of the week. For example, on Sundays, I eat another bowl of Cheerios, snack more in the afternoons, and if my wife has baked-- she is a fabulous cook, and she does her best to make the recipes healthy, using less sugar (often Splenda) and reducing fat by substituting applesauce for shortening, or making an oatmeal pie crust in lieu of the traditional high calorie, high fat version--I might savor more than usual, knowing that these calories I steal will be paid back the next day in the form of a ten miler or speed session.

So the salient points are what you eat and how much. We all know that one of the advantages of racking up all those miles (and the only perceptible one I can imagine) is that it does give license to eat more, again not the quantities of competitive eaters, but more than usual. The body demands it.

I often wonder if I run because it's healthy, it's a competitive outlet, it boosts my self-esteem...or because it allows me to do more of my two of my three favorite activities: eating and sleeping. The third serves no relevance here, but I will admit I've thought about running while both eating and sleeping--dreaming perhaps--but never during sex.

The well-documented drawback of marathon training is that more running translates to less sex. Why? More sleep. Unfortunately, it's a vicious cycle of eating, sleeping and running. And if you're lucky--or resourceful--you can include some amorous activity as well. That alone ought to be one reason to look forward to the marathon and some catch-up time afterward.

Back to food and what to eat during the run. The choices are endless—bars, gels, shots, beans. In short use what works, but use something. And before taking it in a marathon, try it in training. If you've never used gels, don't make the marathon, your hopeful Boston qualifier, your trial run. If you've never tried them, they have the consistency of honey (and are just as sticky) so you need about a quart of water as a chaser. I usually suck down three or four gels per marathon. I wouldn't know why, but it's usually a good six months until I can even think about trying to stomach another Powergel Double latte.

In PP (Pre-Powerbar) days of the 70's and 80's, marathoners had to find other sources of glycogen replacement, but hydration was emphasized more. So, drink the water on the course and that was it. Nothing else. There were no other options at the time, or so it seemed.

Until my fourth marathon--Harrisburg 1985--which could have been my best ever, save for sun and 75 degrees. I was in perhaps my best shape ever and a spry 27 years old. The first 20 miles went great, on a 2:50 pace, then came the bonk. The closing miles weren't pretty. I needed something. At 24, a woman along the Susquehanna Riverfront was handing out root beer barrels and Tootsie Roll pops. I didn't crave the idea of sucking on a lolly while running, but I grabbed a root beer barrel. That bit of sugar and the diversion it created saved me from dwelling on the discomfort. I stumbled to a 49 minute final 10K, just barely breaking three hours. I still look back at that as my "what if" marathon.

The weather that day, on the second Sunday in November, starkly contrasted with the week before when several members of our running club battled a frigid rain at the Marine Corps Marathon. I'm not sure which was worse. I suspect the rain in the days before tech clothing, but the heat was no picnic—and the times reflected that. If only it had been 20 degrees, or even 10 degrees cooler--what if?

When it comes to race fuel and the plethora of choices, one of my pre-run favorites is raisins, which carry much the same punch as the energy chews and manmade choices, including candy. Some sanctimonious foodies would never let candy touch their tongues. Or so they say. I proudly use candy as a running booster, both before and during a run. Along with raisins, I'll would pop a handful of Mike and Ike's before a long run. I know they are mostly sugar and dyes, but they work just as effectively as the energy-beans, which are glorified jelly beans with a higher price tag. Mike and Ike's have been a guilty pleasure for many years, but I have narrowed my consumption to just before long runs.

Since that Harrisburg race, I stuff hard candy in my pockets for every marathon. I do it for training runs as well, and I am amazed at the effect. Part of it may be psychological in the closing miles, but I don't much care to analyze it; I just know it works. One piece of hard candy for every two miles seems to suffice in the final six or less.

Never mind my dentist's recommendation to lay off the hard candy.

Hydration and its Drawbacks

Hydration--or lack thereof--can often spell success or doom in a marathon, particularly if you are lucky enough to run on a summer day so sultry Florida in July might feel more comfortable. Pennsylvania gives us the worst of all worlds: winters that rival the Arctic and summers steamier than the tropics.

So often when you schedule a marathon months in advance, you're taking a huge risk, sometimes regardless of the time of year. That's why hydration is crucial, and it can't start the night before. Too late. Instead, start pumping fluids no less than three days prior to the race. You'll spend that sleepless night before and the early miles of the race paying back the rented water. Been there, done that. Nonetheless, the benefits will stay with you in the final unrelenting miles of the marathon.

The drawback to hydration is the combination of pre-race jitters and a full bladder. Add coffee and the hope of a jolt from caffeine, and you find port-a-johns in short supply. Fortunately, there are usually woods along the early miles most marathon courses, even Boston. Of course, pit stops mean lost time, a less than desirable option when seconds count. Depending on the fullness of the bladder, a guy might sacrifice 30 seconds; a woman, probably more, though I plead ignorance on that. Mark Remy on runnersworld.com calculated the length of a pee break for a man is about 24 seconds. He claims to have accumulated empirical evidence as well as quantitative and qualitative research to reach that conclusion.

During my marathon PR at Boston in 1987, I didn't stop to pee once, but I drank no coffee. I did however, start hydrating the Friday before and didn't stop. It worked, thanks to a cool, damp day in the 50's.

In 2014, when I didn't hydrate well enough, it reached the mid-60's with full sun. In spite of Gatorade at every one of the 22 or 23 water stations along the course, it was too little too late. Not that I crashed completely, but better attention to hydration sooner might have contributed to a somewhat better time. I made sure to correct that in 2015. Rain, windy and temperatures in the low 40's precluded any chance of dehydration, so my four or five gallons of diluted Gatorade in the three days prior to the marathon had me ducking off the road three times to reverse-hydrate. Nonetheless, I still manage to get under my qualifying time--by three seconds in less than adequate shape--but no doubt I'd have been at least a minute faster without the pee breaks. So there are advantages and disadvantages of adequate hydration.

One recent concern brought on by 6-7 hour marathoners who guzzle gallons of water is hyponatremia, or water intoxication. This rare affliction only manifested itself with the proliferation of more marathons and more people who drink far more than what they lose. These are the people whose marathons resemble Sunday strolls. They hear and read about the need for hydration then gulp prodigious volumes of fluid. These are many of the same individuals who eat voraciously expecting the scale to slide to the left but are disappointed to see it go the other way.

For me, water doesn't cut it. I need Gatorade, before, during, and after. If sports drinks cause problems, try diluting them to obtain added fuel the muscles will need late in the race. But again, try whatever fluid replacement you prefer in training before using it race day.

Sleep is Not Weakness

Ah, sleep: peaceful, blissful, energizing. Sleep isn't just for the lazy, though that's been the stigma for generations. The more you sleep, the lazier you are.

Baloney, for lack of something considerably more vulgar!

Thankfully, the Puritanical-bred conviction that sleep is a byproduct of sloth has been relegated to fantasy and fallacy.

Now we know and understand the myriad of benefits sleep provides. In reality, it is for the ambitious. That's not to say too much is beneficial. It's not, but neither is too little. Most Americans are sleep-deprived from stress, working too much, weighing too much, exercising too little, and on and on. These problems have turned slumber into full-fledged medical discipline.

We all experience nights of not falling asleep, waking up, etc. Research, though, confirms that exercise improves sleep quantity and quality. Sometimes six solid, uninterrupted hours is superior to nine wake-filled hours. There are those who can get by just fine on 4-5 hours per night, but that's the exception. Just speculating, but I doubt too many of those people are marathon runners. If they are, they belie conventional wisdom. Or they have some chemical help.

Most experts recommend seven to eight hours per night. I prefer more than that. Maybe nine. Unfortunately, an alarm and a job interfere with that idea of utopian slumber. Nevertheless, nine to ten hours is fairly common among elite runners. Pound out 100 miles per week and there's not much time to do more than rest and refuel. I've read that Ryan Hall schedules daily afternoon naps he labels "business meetings," which in a sense, they are.

The bottom line is if you want to qualify for Boston, or do well in any marathon, don't skimp on sleep. Just remember, though, that how well you sleep the night before your race is insignificant. Anxiety and hydration keep most runners awake much of the night before, but it really doesn't matter. I awoke at three a.m. prior to a recent marathon I ran, and no matter how hard I tried, I couldn't go back to sleep. But I had satisfaction in knowing I had slept well the previous night. In essence, if the marathon is Sunday, aim for a restful and long night of slumber on Friday night. Saturday night won't matter (unless doing some very ill-advised carousing into the wee-hours). You can always make up for the restless night after the race, but that's usually not much better, given the stiffness and aches accumulated running 26.2 miles. A little Ibuprofen isn't a bad idea then.

And something for young runners to look forward to, if you're fortunate enough to enjoy a long running career, racking up miles and training for a marathons for decades, once you get into your fifties, you'll discover that most nights—and mornings—feel like you've just run a marathon.

Finding the Perfect BQ Marathon

Only marathon runners would see the letters BQ and think marathon. Let the bar-b-que (short of a second "B") serve as the post-race treat.

Once you've run at least one marathon to finish and perhaps others to work on improving your time, then you can begin to target the one for your Boston qualifier. The best advice is to identify a race on a flat course or one that boasts a substantial net downhill elevation. Boston itself features a more than 400-foot elevation drop, but it's the several rapid descents that inflict the quad-jarring damage, something to keep in mind when examining possible qualifiers. The B.A.A website lists marathons that boast the highest percentage of Boston qualifiers. The Boston Marathon itself is among them, largely because 70-80% of the runners any given year have qualified, so the 40% re-qualifying rate makes sense. Sort of. One might think more who qualified before should do it again. If marathon running was an exact science that might appear a valid supposition, but there are innumerable variables among the qualifiers. Some are there to celebrate achievement so re-qualifying is not a priority, but the disparity in numbers also says something about the unrelenting elevation changes, and it being a spring marathon and the associated hardship for those in those in northern climes to get in quality training.

Certainly, fall is clearly a better time to run a marathon. The hard runs in the heat of summer toughen a runner, so when the temperatures cool, it's an added boost, both mentally and physically. Thus, it's no coincidence that most of the marathons on the list take place in the fall.

Select a race in late September or October and you may be fortunate enough to qualify for two Bostons, as some people were able to do in 2012. It's not a typical occurrence but it's a bonus when it does.

The B.A.A. typically opens registration the second or third Monday in September. A new qualifying window usually begins that week or the following week. That's not to say you can't run a mid or even late September race and still get in. It just depends on the year. In 2012, Boston didn't fill until early October for 2013. Instances like the 2014 race, and the close to 3,000 qualifiers who didn't get in are unique.

Add that to the closer to 2,000 qualifiers who came up 1:02 short of earning a number for 2015 and it clearly behooves a runner to get as far under the BQ as possible. Don't leave it to chance that just qualifying is good enough to get in. When the goal is to qualify, breaking that required time is all that matters. Boston is the sexy marathon these days. The 2013 bombing only brightened the luster. It won't always be that way.

The B.A.A. promises to review the entry process. One suggestion would be to increase the percentage of qualifiers to 90%. That would require a reduction in charity runners, but when so many legitimate qualifiers are missing out in lieu of several thousand charity participants, there is bound to be questions of fairness. I don't begrudge charity runners. Their efforts are to be lauded and admired. However, there are thousands of other marathons they could use as money-raisers. Sure, Boston is special, but it's also special for those who EARN the privilege to run there.

Depending on your level of frugality, the exuberance of the qualifying for Boston may be quickly dampened by the cost. Entry is currently $175. But no one really cares. It's simple supply and demand. Runner demand is astronomical and supply of spots is limited. As a result, I have no doubt the B.A.A. could charge whatever it wanted and that would deter very few from running.

It was a bit of sticker shock for me when I registered for the 2012 race (entry was a few dollars less that year). I would have been naïve to expect it anywhere near the $40 it cost in 1988. Back then, every runner also needed a TAC number (The Athletics Congress, forerunner of USA Track and Field). That added another $25 onto the cost. Not to mention, gas, food and hotels were cheaper. So was the supplementary apparel (then limited to a painter's hat, short-sleeve t-shirt…jackets were available but rare).

The message if you plan on running Boston is to be financially fit as well. Save for the trip. Traveling from Pennsylvania, I estimate the entire trip usually costs me about $1,100-1,200. That includes my entry fee, meals, hotel, gas, and the jacket and hoodie I buy for myself to go with other shirts for family. It's possible to get off cheaper, and if you make the trip every year, you probably won't buy a jacket annually and you might cut elsewhere, but if Boston is a once-in-a-lifetime experience, save and savor.

Tips for the Run

Start slow. Too many runners get caught up in the hoopla of a marathon, the waving, high-fiving, all the hysterics, all of which might be great in many places, but hey, wait till you *get* to Boston! Too many runners go out as if they're shot from the starting cannon. It might feel great for awhile, but as fast as you go in those opening miles, you'll go just as slow in the closing miles. Think of how many runners are high-fiving spectators at three miles then how many are doing it 23. Save energy, save the enthusiasm. That reserve in the tank will aid you in the closing miles.

Being overly vivacious is not a problem for me. I am a notoriously slow starter. No matter the distance, I need to establish and settle into a pace. The initial mile of most training runs is usually about 10 minutes. It wasn't always that ungodly snail-like, but in my best marathons

I've always purposely made the first mile the slowest. Repeat, the first mile--not the last mile--should be the slowest. If you can accomplish that simple pace inversion, you improve your chance of running a qualifying marathon. But again, there are no guarantees whatsoever in marathon running. Much often depends not so much on training but the runner, the day, and how they mesh once the race begins.

My first year at Boston, with the then imposing field of 5300 runners and no chip timing, it took a minute to cross the starting line, and nine minutes each for the first few miles. I was pissed! Turns out, I didn't realize at the time that was to my benefit. I hit ten miles at a seven minute pace then raced the next 15 in 1:35. Okay, but not tremendously impressive then. Viewed from the lens of today perspective, it was pretty damn awesome!

The crowd's enthusiasm can stoke the adrenalin, but that is like a drug. Don't let it cloud your thinking and purpose. Hold back. Save the legs, the glycogen, and the fluids for the second half. The goal is negative splits (also, the title of my blog on google+--couldn't resist the opportunity for some self-promotion). The ability to run the second half faster than the first will net tremendous rewards.

Possibly the most arduous portion of any marathon is the middle miles. In fact, "The middle miles suck," an apt description I heard just past 12 miles in one recent marathon. The stretch from 6-20 is the worst. Fortunately, most runners mentally divide the race into segments, focusing on small goals—10K, 10 miles, the next water station, etc. But it's like anything else. The middle of anything requiring effort is the most mentally enduring, whether it's the workweek or a marathon. Best advice is just bear it, use the divide and conquer strategy, and before you know it, you're halfway—20 miles.

The last 10K is the marathoner's crucible, and it's guaranteed to hurt. The level and intensity of that pain is determined by the course, weather, effort, and training. If all goes as it should, well-trained runners marvel at the number of competitors they pass, many walking and otherwise falling by the wayside. Serious runners contend the race begins at 20, but it's not just about speed, rather attrition. When I'm running well, I find the most satisfying part of the race is clicking off those final miles and determining how much time I have left to reach my goal. If I start to fade around 25, I know I can push through the final 1.2 miles on willpower and guts, if nothing else.

Then when that finish line comes into view and you're under BQ time, all the work and sacrifice comes to fruition. You have made it. You've reached distance running's pinnacle. You've qualified for the Boston Marathon!

Training Through an Abominable Winter (2014)

Following my inauspicious experiences of the previous two years, I was determined to do it all right in 2014: train well and make to both the starting and finish lines. Winter, however, had other intentions.

Many times I was ready to throw my hands in the air and just give it up. But I could not. I kept harkening back to the immortal line from Shakespeare's Richard III: "Now is the winter of our discontent."

Little did this ruthless king have any idea how much he was dramatically understating this winter and the cursed Polar Vortex across the eastern US.

I hasten to admit it, but I became quite nimble running in snow, avoiding major slips and falls. It wasn't for lacked practice. The demanding conditions--brutal cold, endless snow, occasional ice-- are taxing even the most dedicated runner. It probably wouldn't have bothered me as much if I wasn't training for Boston.

Previous winters when I've been gearing up for Patriot's Day were nowhere near as arduous. The winter of 2012 was downright balmy, so 2013 seemed painstaking, but compared to months of Arctic South in 2014, that was like a Caribbean cruise.

Yet, I had to plow ahead. No pun intended. As pessimistic as I tend to be, I searched—valiantly—for some measures of hope. I kept telling myself that runs in three or four inches of snow, while not fast, were productive. They made runs on dry pavement that much quicker. And tackling fierce head winds and chill factors below zero strengthened my mental resolve. Perhaps I was just deluding myself, but I need whatever encouragement I can muster.

Hints of a warm-up were causes for celebration. Only layering with two pair of gloves instead of three. When it did slightly warm-up into the mid-20s for a day or so, the freezer and the snow machine fired right back up. Warm-ups, thaws, mild temperatures—usual parts for the weather lexicon that took a hiatus. Probably to the Caribbean.

It compelled me to adjusted my goals for Boston, giving up on speed and just putting in the long run. Given my recent history, I just wanted to get to the starting line, then to the finish, regardless of time.

Yes, I did feel discontent, but it was mild. Except during this winter *mild* was a four-letter word rarely uttered.

When I thought no winter could rival the truculence and obstinacy of 2014, then came 2015. I attempted to make it more tolerable with a mid-February vacation in Hawaii (my ultimate retirement home). But that just exacerbated the training frustrating, from temperatures in the teens and wind chills below zero, to afternoon highs in the 80s then back to the frigid reality of central Pennsylvania. While I can't complain about running in the sun and 80s in Waikiki, I wasn't quite used to it, particularly when the humidity crept up a few afternoons and it felt like July at home.

But home, it was 80 degrees colder, not counting the winds. Needless to say, the trip did hamper my Boston training, but I wouldn't trade it. Winter weather was another story, and the primarily reason why I ran about 80 fewer miles than in 2015 and wound up four minutes slower.

A Somewhat Forgettable Time While Having an Unforgettable Time

The winter notwithstanding, I made it to Boston--to the start and to the finish-- but it not quite as smoothly as I had hoped. This was a piece I wrote for my blog, negativesplits. It was also featured in the June 2014 issue of Runner's Gazette.

The dual connotation of time. This year's Boston Marathon ran on connotation, from the many meanings of run, to spirit, to emotion, to success, to achievement, to victory.

The 26.2 mile parade of exaltation and exuberance didn't quite go as planned for me. My GPS watch refused to lock into the satellite so I was forced to intuitively track my pace, just as I did the last time I traversed the sacred Boston course 26 years ago.

Though it didn't seem so at the time, that was a comparatively minor setback, both in my world and that of this great marathon in general.

The past two years I had qualified and made the eight hour drive from central Pennsylvania to Boston, but never made it to the starting line. In 2012, I chose not to bake in the 90 degree April heat and took a deferment, though I ran a marathon that fall to justify my spot. Then in 2013—what some say was fortuitous—I came down with the flu on the drive to Boston and left for home on Marathon Monday just as the race was starting. I recall telling my wife I'd never come back again.

Just over eight hours later, after the bombings, I knew I had to go back--for Boston and for me.

Enduring a Labor Day weekend marathon steam bath in State College, I re-qualified, made the cut-off for the field by a mere 10 seconds, then battled a horrific winter. I felt like Job, metaphorically speaking-- until I caught myself--until I remembered that this marathon wasn't just about me, but about running and about those who support us runners, those innocent bystanders who lost lives and ways of life simply by being there for their running loved ones.

And I had the nerve to think of myself as Job.

Still, I dwell on what I didn't do and what I could have done: my typical marathon postmortem.

Along with my watch, the mid-April sun and temperatures in the mid-60s made for a terrific day for spectators, but a little too much too soon for runners who'd been logging long runs in tights and gloves for the past four months. And the Newton Hills seemed longer than a quarter century ago. But I ground it out, about six minutes slower than I had hoped, but good enough to earn a qualifying spot next year for when I hope the crowds are just as enormous, just as enthusiastic and just as energetic—and I can enjoy them.

As the throngs cheered for me, those I passed, and those passing me, several thoughts crossed my mind. I wanted so much to tap into their contagious energy, but I couldn't, at least not as I had hoped. Perhaps the surrealism of the moment made me too insular. *I'm running the Boston Marathon, in 2014! Why am not into this more?* The question was lost. No discomfort, tightness, nausea or other pain would come close to the inexplicable suffering of those of a year ago. *This is nothing! I got this.* Yes. I HAD it okay, but I wanted to SEIZE it more than I did.

Nevertheless, I can say I was there: Boston 2014, a marathon that shall live forever as the race that not only demonstrated the resiliency of running, the event itself, and Boston as a city, but of the United States and the values we hold true, regardless of what irrational zealots try to do to scare us and disrupt what he treasure and hold precious.

We won, the Marathon won, and Freedom won. On Patriot's Day.

I'm grateful to have been a part of it and earn that cherished medal, one nearly twice the size of the two I earned in the late 80's.

So I accept that my running time wasn't memorable, but the time I had running is a memory that I will many times rewind and savor for all my life.

Team Boston

The Boston Marathon is more than the pre-eminent event in distance running or the crowning jewel of marathoning.

It is a team. Every runner is an alumni member, a devoted fan.

It is no accident that this team concept solidified itself after the 2013 bombing. "Boston Strong" became a ubiquitous rallying cry that crossed currents with all the professional franchises in the city of Boston. The marathon's signature logo appeared next to that of the Red Sox, Bruins and Celtics.

And the marathon outdraws them all— collectively. On one day!

Then there's the gear. While the marathon doesn't possess any kind of uniform for all competitors (the numbers represent that as much as anything) j there are jackets, hoodies, t-shirts, singlets, shoes--all carrying the B.A.A signature unicorn. The volume of Boston Marathon apparel rivals that of any major sports league franchise. And in keeping pace with them, so does the price.

The marathon, like any franchise has its legends and stars. Names like Clarence DeMar, Johnny Kelley, Bill Rodgers, Joan Benoit are to running as Babe Ruth, Ted Williams, and Carl Yastrzemski are to Red Sox fans, Bob Cousy, John Havlichek and Larry Bird are to Celtic fans, and Bobby Orr to Bruins' rooters.

The Boston Athletic Association is the ownership, complete with its management team that determines the criteria for the runners on the team each year. Like that of any sports franchise, it is not without its criticisms, whether about the difficulty of qualifying times, overabundance of charity runners, or race logistics. About the only subject for which the B.A.A. doesn't draw criticism is wins or losses. But give the hardened New

England fans time and they just might conceive of some such way to find fault!

The Boston Marathon team boasts and attracts the best runners nationally and internationally. The B.A.A sets the criteria for its team and reviews and seeds the qualifiers. But no matter where they come from, the fans cheer everyone, though there's no doubt the top American runners hear the loudest accolades.

Team Boston maintains corporate sponsors that keep the event thriving, their logos prominently displayed at the start, finish and in-between. In 2015, the B.A.A and one of those sponsors, adidas, opened Boston Marathon RunBase at the 26 mile mark on Bolyston Street. RunBase is a combination store, marathon museum, and workout area with a locker rooms and an area for workshops, clinics and seminars. It also allows visitors to do a virtual run of any part of the marathon course.

Unique to the marathon is that the stadium, or arena, extends 26.2 miles--the length of the Patriot's Day tailgate party as well—even longer if counting the lengths of the corrals and the finish line area. It is a challenge that requires over five thousand volunteers and lots of paid help.

Unlike other sports, including team tennis, there is no professional running league of teams representing cities and regions. The closest is the Olympics, but that's only once every four years in varied international venues. The Boston Marathon is essentially a team that plays or runs every year at the same time and the same place.—all home events, no road trips (except for the thousands of runners who travel there). Home course advantage exists for those Boston Marathon veterans who have run the course many times, some in upwards of 40+ years in a row. Regardless of their times, there is a section of the race's hall of fame—if such an entity existed—reserved for them, as well as for all the winners.

Best of all, no one on the Boston Marathon team is ever traded or released. The marathon's qualifying times takes care of weeding out those who can no longer compete and welcomes the new qualifiers who meet the standard.

It is a team that embraces all who earn the opportunity to toe the line on Patriot's Day. It's not easy, nor should it be. And that's what makes it most rewarding.

Did I Mention Overtraining?

As I was working on this book, I was training for two marathons, an effort far beyond my capabilities at the time. The result: I felt like I had been pummeled by a two-ton grizzly bear.

Such is the nature of overtraining syndrome, a malady with which I grappled for months before I finally identified it and sought to terminate it.

Writing is challenging enough, but putting down words on a topic I was coming to detest made this work insurmountable, though not quite as much as actual training.

I spent several pages documenting my many travails, including my proclivity toward overdoing it. I know I'm not 30, or 40, or even 50 anymore but I refuse to capitulate to age. So I kept pushing 50-55 mile weeks in June then backed off for a week before resuming. Bear (no pun intended) in mind that I had accumulated nearly 5,000 miles in just over two-and-a-half-years, training for five marathons—and all in my early and mid-50's. I'd gone through bouts before when I'd been able to toss the bear off my back for a time. But in early August, it came down with more ferocity than ever before. The lack of desire to run had deteriorated into near refusal. The bear nearly had to push me out the door. And every run resembled a death march from slow to slower to slowest. My body ached worse than if the bear and I wrestled for hours. Most of the aches were unexplained, though most were due to muscle tightness loosened through repeated sessions on the foam roller. Combine all that with general fatigue, malaise, irritability and I was baffled. Was it depression? I had many of the signs, and I have experienced slight bouts (though now I might re-think that diagnosis).

Most damning was my lack of desire to run. I not only felt little desire to go out, but I wondered what it would be like to not have to do it at all. That's probably not unlike a drug addict contemplating going clean. I'd heard of simple overtraining to or burnout, but this is a diagnosed malady that affects those who run, bike, lift, whatever. And one doesn't need to be doing a large volume of work to suffer from it. In essence, it is what occurs when the body is unable to meet the demands of training, metabolically and restfully.

I couldn't understand why I was unable to maintain the same level of mileage this summer as last, and the year before. I didn't have the long runs and the total mileage, but the intensity was higher. If I'd done it then, why couldn't I do it now?

One point that resonated most with me is that we can't compare ourselves to others. Just the point I tried to impart about training programs: everyone is different. I need to remember that when I'm trying to work harder so I can get faster than other guys in my age group.

As I googled overtraining syndrome, I found hundreds of websites that detail the causes (as if I didn't know), signs, and treatment, which is very simply, REST. I waded through dozens of the more reputable websites and compared my situation to the symptoms. Out of ten listed, eight had infiltrated me. If 12 were listed, I had ten. About the only one I didn't have was loss of weight. Lack of appetite was never an issue. Quite the contrary, in fact.

Locating a diagnosis improved my well-being. But there were these two marathons, one two weeks and another eight weeks away. Both out of the question.

The identification begs the question of when I could expect to start training again. Much depends on how I feel. When I regain the desire to run, that's positive sign, but one I cannot interpret as license to begin doing speed work or long runs. Rather, I must settle for short, easy runs. Or even walking.

Recovery time from this nemesis is directly proportional to the amount of time it took to fester into a colossal affliction—weeks, months, a year. The latter is totally unacceptable. I can deal with weeks, and only if I can run 3-4 days at an easy pace. But a year? No way!

So as I boasted of my resiliency to withstand decades of training, I finally faced my own demise, the falling upon my sword, only figuratively. I take some consolation in knowing that I can bounce back quickly from whatever hits me. I need to take into account I am older (regretfully) and I can't continue to up the ante, to keep trying to outdo last year, when I outdid the year before, and so on. If age was regressive, that might be possible. Lamentably, it is not.

Regardless of age or ability or whatever injury or illness lurks, we are always looking forward to improving—running faster and farther. Nature's lack of cooperation greatly frustrates us, so we try to defy those principles. And wind up sidelined.

In spite of my best efforts to steer you clear of my many physical gaffes and mental miscalculations, you will slip up as well. It is inevitable. But mistakes we make today lay the foundation for the triumphs of tomorrow.

Good running and good luck in your quest for that Boston qualifier.

Gary Ishler

Postscript: After four months of reduced mileage and intensity, I was able to bounce back and train for Boston 2015, mindful that the respite was restorative to my mind and body, and that the line between fitness or failure is one that I approach cautiously and never straddle.

References

Below are sources I consulted most immediately in preparing this book. However, over the past 30-40 years, there are literally hundreds of other books, magazines and websites from which I have gleaned mountains of valuable information. I can't possibly list them all, largely because I've forgotten what I retrieved and culled from where and when. Much of it has become common knowledge, available in multiple locations. With supreme confidence, I can say much came from *Runner's World* during the course of my 32 year uninterrupted subscription (that ought to entitle me to some discount, shouldn't it?)

Boston Athletic Association. *baa.org*. 2014-2015.

--. 2015 Boston Marathon Official Program. *Boston* magazine. 2015.

Burfoot, Amby, Ed. *Runner's World Complete Book of Running*. Emmaus, PA: Rodale Press, Inc., 1997.

Clark, Josh. *Marathon Training Plan and Schedule*. 2014. coolrunning.com. 11 August 2014.

Connelly, Michael. *26.2 Miles to Boston: A Journey into the Heart of the Boston Marathon*. Guilford, CT: Lyons Press, 2014.

Daniels, Jack, Phd. *Daniels' Running Formula Second Edition*. United States of America: Human Kinetics, 2005.

Fixx, James F. *Jim Fixx's Second Book of Running*. New York, NY: Random House, 1978, 1979, 1980.

—. *The Complete Book of Running*. New York, NY: Random House, 1977.

Galloway, Jeff. *Galloway's Book on Running*. Bolinas, CA: Shelter Publications, Inc., 1984.

Pierce, Bill and Scott Murr, and Ray Moss. Runner's World Run Less, Run Faster: Become a Faster, Stronger Runner with the Revolutionary 3-Run-a-Week Training Program *(Revised Edition)*. Emmaus, PA: Rodale, Inc, 2007, 2012.

Runner's World. *runnersworld.com*. 2014.

CPSIA information can be obtained
at www.ICGtesting.com
Printed in the USA
LVOW12s0439030816
498849LV00042B/523/P